BUSINESS BRIEFS

By
Donna Lagorio Montgomery

Published by
St. John's Publishing, Inc.
6824 Oaklawn Avenue, Edina, Minnesota 55435

ISBN 0-938577-18-2

First Edition 0 9 8 7 6 5 4 3 2 1

BUSINESS BRIEFS

To employers and employees
who realize that when people come first,
a company prospers.

BUSINESS BRIEFS

BUSINESS BRIEFS

Finding Happiness at Work

1. Organizations consist of individuals, not groups of people. Therefore, individuals should be primary.

2. When businesses are young and growing, employers are sometimes so rushed they become caretakers only, forgetting to take care of their most valuable asset: employees.

3. With the pressure of business matters on an employer's brain, people relationships are often ignored.

4. When management thinks of employees and their happiness first, productivity rises.

5. Workers will put up with a lot of discomfort and make many sacrifices, if they feel their efforts are appreciated by employers.

6. Start-up years and difficult times can limit the amount of money businesses pay employees, but if an employer is open and honest, and identifies the problem, employees are usually supportive.

7. Employers and public officials lose support when they give themselves huge raises in financially difficult times, then expect employees to accept delays in pay raises, take pay cuts, or otherwise tighten belts and struggle to provide for their growing families.

8. Employees need to see employers tighten their own belts first, delay their own pay raises, and be first to take pay cuts in hard times.

9. Employees remember what employers often forget, that each has a unique personality and separate life outside the office.

10. Unfortunately, the motivation that keeps many employees coming to work each day, rain or shine, is money, not job satisfaction.

11. If money is the only incentive keeping employees on the job, they'll probably quit the moment a better offer comes along. With the labor shortage increasing daily, businesses won't survive if they can't keep employees.

12. Employers have to make the work environment pleasant enough for employees to enjoy their jobs.

13. When employers are respectful, employees are happy and enjoy coming to work; also, productivity improves.

14. It seems more waking hours are spent at a job than at home. Parents often leave for work before children are up, come home at supper time, or after kids are in bed. No wonder some workers, especially mothers, feel harried, guilty, and inefficient at home and work.

15. Given the number of hours a person works away from home, it makes good sense for the workplace to be as pleasant as possible.

16. Words employers and employees say to each other, or gestures they use, may seem unimportant, but kind words and thoughtful gestures are essential, bonding, and rarely forgotten.

17. A job atmosphere that accommodates employees' dual roles and responsibilities as workers and parents, minimizes adverse feelings and productivity failings.

Workers Need Encouragement

18. When self-esteem is a priority, creativity flourishes.

19. Creativity needs to be encouraged. Employers and supervisors should get out of the way and let employees determine how best to do a job.

20. If employees realize their special talents and labors are appreciated, they'll come up with extraordinary ideas. They'll also begin to feel they're important, and will work harder to help the company grow.

BUSINESS BRIEFS

21. Workers need to be recognized, not ignored. They need encouragement and help from co-workers and employers to cope with job pressures, high prices, shrinking incomes, illnesses, family problems, and other difficulties.

22. The workplace takes so many hours from workers' lives, there needs to be a strong support system to help them survive.

23. Creative and inventive workers are a bonus for the company. Wise employers encourage workers to be the best they can be.

24. Employees who work in progressive environments and receive positive encouragement on a daily basis, will work wonders for their employers.

25. Each member of a work team has unique gifts and talents.

26. There's not a person alive who doesn't have a special gift for others. In an organization, an employee's gifts can help a company grow, improve working conditions, or bring other benefits.

27. Employers must find each employee's gifts and talents to nurture them and encourage their productive use.

Appreciating the Workplace

28. The workplace can be as exciting and stimulating, depressing and mellow as workers and employers want it to be.

29. Employees can compete for their employer's favor, or they can cooperate to make their workplace pleasant each workday.

30. Whether a new or promoted employee, each should be helped by co-workers.

31. Workers need to realize that bickering doesn't solve problems, get work done, or win over employers. It creates difficulties and disappointments.

32. Peaceful and pleasant work surroundings contribute to an employee's career growth.

33. Businesses aren't battlegrounds where half the employees are enemies of the other half. That indicates bad management.

34. Good managers lead by example, encouraging employees to set and achieve their own goals.

35. Good managers encourage employees to cooperate with each other and acquire an appreciation for working.

36. Employers who keep aware of employees' needs and attempt to satisfy them, are good managers and good examples.

Smelling the Roses

37. By the time kids are sixteen, they're legally able to get a job. When their leisure time is drastically reduced, they quickly realize what a precious gift their leisure time is.

38. After young men and women are initiated into the working world, advancing their careers and increasing their income become major goals. Unfortunately, they too often forget to take time to enjoy life.

39. Whether at home or work, people should take time to smell the roses.

40. What co-workers do for entertainment or fun can be quite revealing.

41. Take time out during busy days to communicate with others and catch up on the news.

42. It's fun to share discoveries with co-workers, families, and neighbors.

43. We must never lose track of why we're working. We work for job satisfaction as well as money. Money needn't be an end in itself; it's only a means of support in a world where beautiful sights and experiences are free and begging to be enjoyed.

Acquiring a Sense of Humor

44. No matter what kind of job, it's easier and less annoying when workers have a sense of humor, or when humor is used to defuse angry confrontations.

45. A sense of humor is best when we're able to laugh at ourselves.

46. It's essential to develop a sense of humor to lighten burdens of everyday living.

47. It's usually safer to laugh at situations rather than people. Also, having a sense of humor can relieve tense situations and bring harmony to the workplace.

48. Humor helps workers get through difficult days and troublesome incidents.

 Business Briefs

49. Since many people spend most of their waking hours working, it seems logical that the workplace be as relaxed and happy a place as possible, especially for good health and well-being.

50. Happy people are usually mentally and physically healthy. Workers who go home happy each night after a pleasant day working, make their families happier and return to work happier.

51. Too often workers leave their workplace unhappy, fight traffic all the way home, yell at their families, go to bed angry, awake unrefreshed, then repeat the agonizing process all over again.

52. A kind word is a wonderful gift. A kind word with a twist of humor makes life more enjoyable.

Workers Should Fit the Job

53. When beginning a business career, employees travel a road filled with many potholes, washouts, burnouts, breakdowns, and accidents, any of which may lead to other roads.

54. If you ask people with many years' business experience to share some hindsight, you'll often learn that ups and downs didn't embitter them; instead, they forged a rich and varied resume of experience and accomplishment.

55. Not many people work for one company all their career, or move up the corporate ladder with a steady, straightforward climb.

56. If workers review past experiences, they'll probably recall a few failures along the way that were seemingly disastrous at the time, but when viewed in hindsight, turned out to be stepping stones to a better situation or improved condition.

57. The job or career originally selected may be completely unrelated to what we actually end up doing.

58. We know children change career choices; otherwise, 90% of the world would be crowded with firemen and nurses. Adults can change careers, too.

59. New ideas, new situations, and new challenges make life interesting, exciting, and worthwhile.

60. Conscientious employers are aware of changing circumstances and adjust to them.

61. Wise employers realize employees will grow in knowledge and experience, and be ready for change.

62. If employees can develop and advance where they work, they won't find it necessary to look at other pastures to see if they're greener. Also, employers won't have to keep training new workers.

63. Employers who respect and treasure employees, will make sure employees and their jobs are a good match.

Getting Into Business

64. Wouldn't it be wonderful if we could maintain the enthusiasm we brought to our first full-time job?

65. What destroys our enthusiasm? Why doesn't it last throughout our entire career? Why can't we keep our dream going?

66. Employees mirror each other.

67. If bright, happy, enthusiastic new employees are dejected after working for a company a short time, it's time the company looked within its four walls to find out what squashed employee enthusiasm.

68. When enthusiasm is destroyed in a home, parents are usually responsible. Instead of listening to children's dreams and encouraging them, parents do too much talking or are constantly asserting themselves. A child with initiative is forced to fit into a confining structure and told to avoid changes. Isn't this true in business, too?

69. Often a new employee, a conscientious, enthusiastic, dreamer of dreams, is criticized, pressured, and humiliated until forced into an old, inefficient, misshapen mold we call the corporate structure.

70. Workers' first job and employer are always remembered, good or bad.

71. Companies are first of all, people. Destruction of even one human spirit for conformity's sake adversely affects the company.

72. Companies must allow for individual differences and nurture sparks of initiative and enthusiasm. Survival of business and society depends on it.

Working Versus At-Home Parents

73. Whichever role women choose, wage-earner or homemaker, society makes them feel guilty.

74. It's a new age for employers; mothers are working outside the home. Businesses recognizing and acting on this fact, plus the fact that happy families make happy, productive workers, and vice-versa, have a big advantage.

"Well I bake a mean batch of chocolate chip cookies."

75. A business's secret to success is adaptability.

76. The babies and young children of today's working mothers will be affected by today's decisions when they grow up and enter the workplace. Current employer decisions can have their most dramatic effect on future workers.

77. For the good of all businesses, the welfare of each employee's family should be given priority. If one or both parents work, the jobs of each should be respected and tailored to fit, including start/stop times.

78. Situations constantly change. Jobs that seem right for a family at one period of life, might not be at another. Also, what's right for one family, might not be right for another.

79. It's good for everyone to be flexible, especially businesses.

80. In the new age of women working outside the home, particularly those with children, it's especially important that businesses strive to keep these women happy, whether by innovative work scheduling, workplace improvements, or kind words.

81. Happy mothers can be a business's secret weapon.

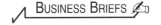

Nursing Good Feelings

82. The workplace shouldn't be a babysitter for employees' personal lives; it should create good attitudes and support.

83. How we're treated by our families is how we tend to treat co-workers in business and others elsewhere.

84. Family tattletales are usually troublemakers at work, while family givers are usually givers at work. Uncomplaining persons at home are usually a joy at the office.

85. The image a CEO has is the image employees mirror back.

86. Businesses encouraging each employee's happiness and job fulfillment are demonstrating a desire to help employees feel good about their jobs and succeed in their careers.

87. Encouraging good feelings begins at home and transfers to the job. It's hard to have good relationships in one place only.

Changing Behavior for the Better

88. People must learn to be responsible for their behavior and its consequences.

89. By being accessible and visible, employers and managers create a helpful atmosphere.

90. Bad behavior problems uncorrected in childhood become problems for co-workers.

91. Employers must solve problems of workplace decency and justice.

92. If expected behavior is verbally reviewed with new employees, they'll know what's expected of them.

93. A workplace is rewarding when employees help each other, boost co-workers' morale, and nurture each other's self-esteem.

Building Self-Esteem

94. Employers achieve amazing improvements in productivity by building self-esteem in employees.

95. Everyone needs recognition.

96. What about a personal letter from the company president for a job well done? Tangible praise is wonderful.

97. Let employees set their own accomplishment goals, then get out of the way so they can achieve them.

98. Employees know their talents better than anyone else, so let them use them.

99. Good employers build employee self-esteem.

100. Employees can make a company great.

101. Good people relationships in a company make for customer loyalty. Unhappy employees flash caution lights and turn customers away.

102. Building employee self-esteem is the key to attracting customers as well as new employees. It's essential to growing a company.

New Employees

103. Hiring employees for their first or a new job is
a tremendous responsibility. First impressions
are lasting.

104. New employees are hopeful, fearful, and filled
with visions. Few regard their jobs as stepping
stones to success elsewhere; they regard them as
the beginning of growth at the present company.

105. New employees see themselves as important contributors to their company's well-being and growth. They don't plan to job hop.

106. New employees bring enthusiasm to their jobs.

107. For a honeymoon period, new employees are like clay: soft and pliable, ready to be molded. After learning the ropes, they develop a new sense of self-esteem and confidence. Otherwise they become disenchanted and acquire low self-esteem.

108. If an employer has competent, respectful managers, new people should find their jobs challenging, exciting, and rewarding. If not, they'll soon look elsewhere for employment.

Creating a Scene

109. If an employee becomes a problem, removal from the public spotlight is recommended.

110. Never discipline an employee in front of others, or where your conversation can be overheard by others.

111. Firing an employee isn't always the best solution.

112. The workplace is actually part of an employee's extended family. Employers and employees must care for each other.

113. It's not enough to support each other in good times. Support has to be part of everyday working relationships in bad times, too.

114. Everyone needs support in times of crisis. When a person creates a scene at work, respond by inviting that person to a private place, then listen quietly, and offer advice and help if wanted.

Being Creative

115. Creativity should be encouraged in everyone.

116. Because a job has always been done one way, doesn't mean it has to be done that way forever.

117. Creativity is the mother of change. Employees have it; employers need to nurture it.

118. Creativity should be encouraged and supported among customers as well.

119. If an employer openly asks for suggestions from customers and employees, says they're important, yet refuses to take them seriously or acknowledge them, then creativity isn't being rewarded, and the business will eventually fail.

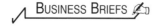

Backbiting and Name-Calling

120. Deal directly with gossips, backbiters, and slanderers by confronting them with facts.

121. Namecalling and backbiting are often the result of jealousy.

122. In offices where good employee relationships are being destroyed, managers need training in employee relations and problem-solving.

123. When problems are openly discussed without any threat to an employee's job, solutions are more easily achieved.

124. Instead of firing employees, conscientious problem-solving and reconciliation are musts for peaceful settlement of conflicts, disputes, and other problems.

125. Verbal abuse destroys too many relationships, because cruel words spoken in anger are difficult to take back and rarely forgotten.

126. Cruel words can be terribly painful. Like deep cuts in the skin, the hurt of cruel words may eventually go away, but they always leave an ugly scar.

127. Backbiting and namecalling must be eliminated from our lives.

128. We need to love and nurture one another, not destroy co-workers, families, and ourselves with a careless mouth.

Getting Employees Working

129. A job should be as much fun as a day off. It should be so exciting to anticipate, that when we wake up in the morning we can hardly wait for our day to begin.

130. People who declare their unquenchable, undying, unmitigated love for their jobs are usually theater people.

131. Allowing employees to project feelings, receive applause for a job well done, and gain recognition from peers and the public, are keys to job enrichment we can learn from the theater.

132. When jobs become exciting and fun to look forward to each day, employers won't have to worry about getting employees to work; employees will be anxious to meet every new challenge and have fun doing it.

Running Away to Another Job

133. If employees are encouraged to discuss and solve work problems at work, they won't run away to different jobs.

134. If employers helped employees solve job problems at work, families wouldn't be subjected to explosions of anger and abuse at home.

# BUSINESS BRIEFS

135. Employers need an open door policy to help employees.

136. Workers run away to different jobs because they're unhappy with what they're doing.

137. Changing jobs is difficult and traumatic; employees don't like changing. They'd rather stay put. Psychologically, physically, and economically, it takes a long time to recover from job changes.

138. When job turnover becomes a major problem and expense, the first logical step is to look at management. Managers determine quality of life in the work place.

139. Employees mirror the image management creates. Improve management's image and you improve workplace quality of life and the way employees treat customers.

Settling Arguments

140. Employees usually have excellent ideas. Unfortunately, they're seldom given the opportunity to use them in solving workplace problems.

141. Encouraging employees to solve problems, with management's help when needed, teaches employees problem-solving.

142. The solution to workplace arguments shouldn't be firing employees. Those involved are better served if problems are discussed and solved openly and equitably.

143. Workplace peace is crucial, because time and lives are too short and important to waste on bickering.

Avoiding Trouble

144. Employees learn from good or bad example. Management sets the example by creating an upbeat or depressing workplace.

145. If employees' good work is recognized and rewarded, they won't attempt to promote themselves by discrediting co-workers.

146. If good work is rarely recognized or rewarded, causing trouble may be the only way employees feel they can get attention.

147. Work boundaries and responsibilities must be clearly drawn.

148. Life is short and precious; there's not enough time to waste it fighting, backstabbing, or gossiping. All employees are important, and have the right to be happy and fulfilled in their chosen vocation or career.

Promoting Arts, Sciences, and Community Events

149. Employees can enrich their lives with art, music, theater, and other cultural pursuits, and businesses have the opportunity to be enrichers by sponsoring or supporting such pursuits.

150. Often, business support is the deciding factor for survival of community art events. When businesses support the arts, customers gratefully support the businesses, and businesses realize a tax break for their support.

Homework

151. The insatiable quest for money, power, recognition, position, or other vanity, propels some workaholics towards their ever-elusive goal to the detriment of their families, co-workers, and others.

152. Employees who constantly have homework are living on disaster's edge and need to change. Not only is their health in jeopardy, but the happiness of family and co-workers is being destroyed.

153. All too late, workaholics realize their children have grown up and left home, and their families have missed the joys of living and growing together.

154. Office work should be done in the office; precious evening hours should be reserved for home and family, the most important homework employees have.

BUSINESS BRIEFS

Evaluating Management

155. Employee morale and productivity improve when management prepares employees for promotions. Also important is employer and employee sharing of ideas and suggestions about long-range goals and individual needs and objectives.

156. As the national labor shortage grows, dishonest, inefficient, and poorly managed companies will disappear.

157. No single member of a family or group is less important than any other. Therefore, let each be treated equitably.

158. Management should do unto others as they would like others to do unto them.

159. If management sets a good example, so will others.

160. Employees thrive on recognition and praise for a job well done.

Sex Education and Ethics in the Office

161. When we talk about sex education and ethics in school and family, two words surface repeatedly: responsibility and consequences. They apply to the workplace, too.

162. Businesses without good ethics won't survive long. If the marketplace doesn't bring them down, employees will.

163. A hang-over from the 1960's seems to be the theory that a person must "do one's own thing." Therefore, since we're supposedly unable to control our actions, we're in no way responsible for them or the consequences. Rubbish!

164. What sets human beings apart from plants and animals is the intangible element called free will. Another intangible element is conscience. We tend to use one and forget the other.

165. We're free, which means we're fully responsible for moral or immoral choices we make. Hopefully, we'll always make moral choices.

BUSINESS BRIEFS

166. Whether at home, office, school or in the community, free will, conscience, morality, and immorality don't change. When people respect the family as a basic and sacred unit of society to be nurtured and supported, rather than undermined, they reaffirm their morality, reinforce their good character, and re-establish their responsible behavior as an example for others.

One More in the Workplace Does Matter

167. People in small businesses must wear many hats, but there comes a time when the hard decision has to be made as to whether a business stays small or is allowed to grow. Both ways have advantages.

168. When businesses experience expansion pressures, employees are usually overlooked. If employees don't complain, their work keeps piling up until they either drown or abandon ship.

169. Businesses in the expansion stage give employees important feedback about management. Employees who are happy in their jobs will temporarily accept extra work to help out, but not indefinitely.

 BUSINESS BRIEFS

170. If employees start early, work late, and bring the office home with them, it's time to ease the workload by hiring more workers.

171. It's unfair to take advantage of a respected and conscientious employee's good humor, graciousness, and love for work. Even if an employee receives a bonus for extra work, such work will eventually become physically unbearable and destructive.

Office Parenting

172. It's wise for business executives to let employees develop their own potential, so it can be put to the most appropriate service for the company.

173. Bigger companies should provide opportunities for employees to try various jobs in search of the best fit.

174. If employees are afraid of taking chances or making bad decisions, they won't want to be very innovative. When that happens, creative employees have two choices: conform or find another job.

175. Every job, even the most structured, should encourage and nurture creativity.

176. The day there's no room for improvement, a job is unchallenging and life becomes boring. To avoid losing a valuable employee, change is needed.

177. No one ever said work must be drudgery.

Next Door Neighbor Business

178. There should be a special community friendship for local businesses, like good relationships neighbors share.

179. As a small neighborhood business grows, the people it employs are in for quite an experience: they'll probably learn most of the jobs.

BUSINESS BRIEFS

180. Employees with initiative and enthusiasm will benefit and advance, even in a small business.

181. Small business owners are survivors; they have to be, because few banks will help them when times are tough. If small business owners fail, you'll soon find them starting another business.

182. Most small business owners are usually on their own, and really, that's the way most prefer it.

Keeping Your Cool

183. Whether dealing with teenagers as an employer or a parent, the rule is the same: keep your cool. Adults who can't relax and respect teenagers won't earn loyalty.

184. Teenagers don't respond well when yelled at, dehumanized, or talked down to. Who does?

185. Teens have a strong sense of justice and can exceed an adult's expectations, but they must be treated with respect and good humor.

186. Teenagers' first priorities, if they're still in school, are not their jobs and shouldn't be. First and foremost they're students.

187. Employers hiring teenage students part time will be successful by keeping flexible. Everyone will be happier if the number of teens employed is increased, so the number of hours worked per week can be decreased per teen to avoid excessive work.

188. Employers can't realistically expect teenagers to give up their prom or other major school event or sports participation, just to help a company in a two-hour pinch. Family and school should take precedence over employment.

189. An important perk for employees, especially teenagers, is a happy atmosphere. Many teens go through difficult times at home. For those teens, especially, it's important to have a pleasant work atmosphere.

190. Employers who establish pleasant working conditions will get peak output from both teenage and adult workers.

191. When teens are treated respectfully, patiently, and cheerfully, that message comes through loud and clear, and they'll perform 150%.

192. Whether adults, teenagers, grade-schoolers, or pre-schoolers, a good rule to follow is be fair, flexible, friendly, and fun.

Fun Versus Business

193. If a business isn't at least a little bit fun, employees will come and go fast, and the high turnover will be costly and destructive.

194. Teenage workers aren't young at heart, they're just plain young. To understand young workers, older folks should remember their own youth.

195. Recalling happy job memories usually involves something other than the work experience.

196. When employers cast their bread upon the waters, it comes back a hundred-fold. Kindnesses shown teenagers are never lost. Keeping a company's work atmosphere upbeat, happy, and fun, keeps teenagers eager to work for that company.

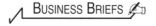

Music in the Office or on the Phone

197. Have you ever been put on hold and had a radio station piped into your phone with a bombardment of commercials? Have you ever become so frustrated you just hung up and decided to call back later? Did you bother to call back at all? Putting customers on hold is a quick way to dissolve a business, especially if the call is long-distance.

198. Forget music and piped-in radio! Most callers on hold prefer an occasional reminder from the operator that the line is still busy. Don't upset customers by forcing them to listen to unwanted music or radio commercials.

199. For some reason we're reluctant to let our minds think freely for more than a short period of time.

200. Silence can be deafening when creative ideas are allowed to flow inside us.

201. People alone in their homes may be free to listen to loud, cacophonous music or turn it off; employees in the workplace aren't.

202. Employees who find it hard to concentrate without music, can always use radios with earphones. That way, employees needing music can have it, while those needing quiet can have it.

Walking Into the Face of the Canon

203. Young part-time employees are often full-time students whose jobs have little to do with their professional goals. If employers can't accommodate them after graduation, they'll work elsewhere.

204. After formal schooling, young people experience fears and anxieties of unemployment, job hunting, and performance on a new job. Also, they usually rank at the bottom, and their self-esteem may be at an all-time low. Employer encouragement is needed more than ever.

205. Employers are responsible for (a) paying employees a living wage; (b) rewarding employees with thanks and recognition for jobs well done; (c) providing employees a happy workplace; (d) giving employees jobs they're happy, qualified, and trained to do; (e) keeping employees challenged and motivated with regular advancements and compensation increases; and (f) protecting employees with competitive insurance coverage and other benefits.

206. An employer is responsible for the physical, mental, and social well-being of employees, and no one ever said it was easy.

Working with Workplace Cliques

207. People thrive on love and recognition; employees are no exception.

208. People need recognition of their talents. Being accepted by peers is important, too.

209. Workplace caring and sharing is essential; cliques are devastating to employees who aren't accepted. Workers are all on the same team and should behave that way.

210. To remind ourselves how painful exclusion can be, we should recall our own school days and kids who were excluded. Even more painful is to recall when we were among the excluded.

BUSINESS BRIEFS

211. Take time to learn more about co-workers,
care for them, and help them. Everyone has
problems. Unfortunately, too many are expert at
hiding them.

212. To stop lies from spreading, carefully correct
gossips attempting to undermine co-workers.

213. Workers won't have regrets if they avoid cliquish behavior. Cliques corrupt workplace loyalties and destroy workplace morale.

214. The role of employers is to establish and maintain high morale and camaraderie among those they serve.

215. It's the employer's job to establish and maintain employee morale.

216. Cliques, whether formed in schools, neighborhoods, or the workplace, are harmful and exclusionary by nature. They should be completely eliminated.

Putting Up with the Pecking Order

217. Business pecking order: CEOs peck VPs; VPs peck directors; directors peck managers; managers peck workers; workers peck each other. Then worker goes home and pecks spouse, spouse yells at children, children kick dog, dog bites cat, cat chases rat, rat runs into trap!

218. Everyone is first nestled in the family. If children are loved and nurtured, there's a chance they'll get a good start. If they can live peacefully in their families, neighborhoods, and communities, they'll have a good foundation for the business world.

219. There has to be continuing love and support outside the home if people are to grow and develop well at their workplace.

220. It takes only one unjust employee to create miserable working conditions for co-workers and perpetuate a morale-destroying workplace.

221. Orderly, respectful relationships are the result of orderly, respectful employees.

222. Each person is important to the successful operation of any organization.

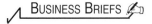

223. When systems break down, an objective, outside consultant may be needed. The problem can be anywhere in the pecking order from the top down or bottom up.

Understanding Absenteeism

224. Employee unhappiness contributes to workplace absenteeism. Such unhappiness should be recognized and remedied because of the double whammy it creates.

225. Workers unhappy in their jobs may develop real illness to avoid working. They may also fail to realize they're unhappy, and that their unhappiness is causing real illness.

226. Since parents' first priority is their children's welfare, employers should establish company policy to accommodate this fact. It's an easy problem to solve, requiring only a written statement allowing parents time off to care for sick children.

227. Parents tend to be honest and conscientious about employment privileges and rights allowing time off to care for sick children. They know they'd hurt themselves if they took unfair advantage of employers.

228. Absenteeism can occur when unhappy employees, bored or dissatisfied with their work, boldly take time off to search for a new job.

229. A kind comment in the privacy of a supervisor's office can convince a troubled employee someone cares. This may be all the employee needs to eliminate absenteeism.

230. If employees are bored, management should take a closer look at the work itself. Maybe bored employees could be transferred to more challenging work. Why not ask them what they'd like to do.

231. Work needn't be fun all the time, but it should certainly be cordial, friendly, and stimulating.

What to Do When Employees Think They're Smarter Than the Boss

232. Find out if it's true!

233. Employees may be smarter than their bosses
in many ways. Wise employers will be
quick to recognize this and structure jobs to help
employees become more challenged.

BUSINESS BRIEFS

234. Small business owners should know their jobs enough to have a working knowledge of each one. If they're weak in some areas, hiring an employee who has the needed skills makes good sense.

235. Highly skilled employees are hired to do highly specific jobs; supervisors should be smart enough to get out of the way.

236. An employee's ideas should be welcomed and appreciated; always.

237. Take time to listen to employees ideas, and thank them for caring.

238. Employers may listen to hundreds of employee ideas before getting a major one, or they may get one immediately. Either way, ideas are important, because who knows a better way of doing a job than the employee doing it?

239. Employers should encourage employees to be creative and look for better ways of doing their job.

240. If employees aren't encouraged to be creative or to share new ideas, where's the fun in a job?

241. Employees encouraged to think for themselves become the pride of their companies.

242. Employees not encouraged to think for themselves drop out, and the turnover becomes costly.

243. Nurturing, encouragement, and recognition
develop steady, loyal, confident, and innovative
employees who are smarter than their bosses; or
so smart bosses let them think.

Encouraging Workers to Save

244. Question: What do working students do with their money? Answer: Some have charge accounts maxed out; some eat their way through paychecks; and some spend heavy on entertainment; few save.

245. Young workers need to understand and anticipate future financial needs, construct a budget, develop a sound savings program, keep debt to a minimum, and save a portion of each paycheck.

246. Whether their salary stays the same or they get a raise, most employees tend to spend what they make. So, "out of sight, out of mind," seems to be a good rule.

When in Doubt, Get the Whole Story

247. Everyone has bad days, bad years, and bad times. Neither employers or employees should condemn someone who's having difficulties or annoying others. It's necessary to know the whole story, and it should be verified before any action is taken.

 BUSINESS BRIEFS

248. A loving family, kind employer, and concerned co-workers can help troubled employees by simply being good listeners.

249. We should be alert to needs of co-workers, lending them a helping hand or ear whenever possible.

Telephone Courtesy & Informing Others About One's Whereabouts

250. Some businesses and professions require employers and employees to tell their offices how they can be reached at all times. Whether sales professionals, doctors, dentists, CEOs or lawyers, it's important to keep receptionists and associates informed.

 BUSINESS BRIEFS

251. No one knows when an emergency may arise requiring someone to be located, so it's basic courtesy to tell someone where you're going, when you plan to return, and how you can be reached in an emergency.

252. *Caller:* Give name, business association, and person with whom you wish to speak.

253. *Receptionist:* Tell caller if the person being called is busy *before* inquiring who is calling.

254. It may be a shock, but fundamental for home and business, that the person called is no more important than the caller. Answer your calls!

255. Time of the person being called isn't more valuable than the caller's time.

256. Don't be evasive or put on airs when dealing with people, especially on the telephone. Simply tell the truth and let people know your whereabouts or what you need or want.

Pros and Cons of Long Weekends

257. Pros and cons of taking long weekends depend on what you're like when you come home after a day's work? Are you a giver or taker?

258. If an employee is kind and lovable at work, but comes home and blows off frustrations on the family, long weekends can be severe punishment to those forced into the role of dog who gets kicked.

259. If something special is planned for family and friends over a long weekend, yard, housework, and other chores should be done another time.

260. No matter how permanent situations seem, people and circumstances can change overnight, sometimes in seconds.

261. We need to spend time with those we love, even if it means doing small things like taking a spontaneous walk together.

262. Employers can be givers, too, and in a way that doesn't require added cost. For example, an employer can calculate an employee's raise to provide a portion as a paid "floating" holiday, usable for a long weekend.

263. Nothing is more important in our brief lives than people, especially those with whom we live and work. As long as we put people first and things last, we'll be on the right track.

264. Long weekends are for enjoying those we love. We mustn't waste such opportunities, because once gone, they're gone forever. If parents don't enjoy children when they're young, they'll have no one to blame but themselves when children grow up and reject them.

Setting a Good Example

265. Whether small matters or big concerns, management must set a good example.

266. Employees can't be told to do as management *says*, because they'll almost always do as management *does*.

267. We forget that businesses are made up of individuals working together for their common good. Instead, we think of businesses as wage earner groups working to benefit owners.

268. Many young people regard older workers as outdated, stodgy, or deadwood, simply because their employers do.

269. Years of experience and uncommon expertise of mature workers should earn them higher wages. However, when employers fire them, the dishonest reason often given is, "You're overqualified." Actually, the real reason is employers won't pay higher wages for higher productivity.

270. When employers fire older workers for unethical reasons, the lesson for young workers is never trust an employer.

"Our organizational planning specialists consider you a prime candidate for an alternative opportunity in the upcoming human resource readjustment implementation."

271. When employers become hardened and corrupt, young workers are influenced to become hardened and corrupt also.

272. Employers must take initiative to change for the better and become ethical and trustworthy. Like it or not, they're role models young workers imitate.

Controlling Anger; Forgiving Mistakes

273. If someone has a grievance against us, we must go get reconciled with that person as soon as possible.

274. Why is it so many people today think religion, ethics, and morality aren't essential to business? Why do they attend religious services on Saturday or Sunday, then tuck morality away the rest of the week?

275. Management determines a company's code of ethics, not only by policies, but also example, good or bad.

276. Employees subjected to unfair outbursts of anger may react by yelling back, quaking in fear, reacting sympathetically, or ignoring the outburst. However, the offending culprit should apologize and be required to ask for forgiveness.

277. Customers subjected to employee anger, rudeness, or indifference, are usually gone before an apology can be given. Since dissatisfied customers tell others, damage is usually permanent and translates to lost revenue from lost sales. If a company loses large numbers of customers it soon goes out of business.

278. Whatever happened to the good old values of politeness and kindness? Consumers aren't getting courteous service; employees paid to serve the public, don't; nobody seems to care.

279. No business can survive by consistently giving bad service.

280. Nearly everyone gets angry sometime. It's not the end of the world. Like anything else, however, anger is temporary. It's natural to express anger, but it should be directed at the right target in a constructive way.

281. In business as in life, when we err, we must ask for forgiveness. Let's also remember when asked to forgive, it's noble to do so.

Eliminating Jealousy

282. People have a knack for getting into trouble. It's not limited to family, school, work, or other place or time of life. It's universal, crossing social, political, and family barriers. Too often it's caused by petty jealousies.

283. When people reflect on their setbacks, they often discover someone's jealousy is the cause.

284. Arguments often start when someone isn't happy with income, especially when compared to someone else's.

285. Jealousy causes problems in the workplace; employees gang up on successful co-workers to discredit them and steal their achievements, promotions, even their jobs.

286. If workers in business are praised, supported, promoted, and paid a just wage, they'll have little reason to be jealous.

287. Fairness eliminates much jealousy.

288. Good managers play no favorites and don't discriminate.

"That was very impressive, Miss Jones, but my daughter has already applied for the position."

289. We're all in this world together and need each other's support. We also need heroes to look up to: people we can admire, not envy. Are supervisors, foremen, middle managers, VPs, and CEOs these role models?

290. Employees imitate supervisors, so supervisors should always set a good example, preventing jealousies by treating employees fairly.

Handling Rejection

291. People in other occupations can learn from those in the performing arts not to take rejection personally and to be gracious in response. Don't burn bridges you may need later.

292. When it comes to overcoming rejection and resiliency, our hats go off to the backbone of our economy: salespeople.

293. Salespeople seem to be open-season and easy game for everyone. If a prospective customer has a bad day, God help the next salesperson who calls.

294. Rejection is part of everyday life, and although it's negative and discouraging, it can be handled in positive, upbeat, optimistic ways.

295. Bankruptcy is treated lightly by those who use it regularly to dodge debts. But to honest persons it represents personal rejection and failure of devastating proportions.

296. Whenever choosing one course of action, we reject others. Each decision we make rejects alternatives. Acceptance of one idea or thing means rejection of others not accepted. Rejection is part of life. What's important is to be gracious, resilient, and not take it personally.

 BUSINESS BRIEFS

Sharing Unemployment with Children

297. Children should be informed of a family crisis such as unemployment. They don't need to know every detail, but should know something about what's happening to help them understand the difficult time.

298. It's important children be informed of a family crisis so they know their parents are dealing successfully with life's difficulties.

299. Caring and sharing parents should help children realize that hard times will pass, just as they did for mom and dad.

Making Wise Judgments

300. Good judgment helps us form opinions objectively and wisely. With bad judgment, we don't form opinions objectively or wisely. Each day we form many opinions. Hopefully, they'll be objective and wise, reflecting good judgment.

BUSINESS BRIEFS

301. At the workplace, decisions have to be made daily. Those who consistently make rational decisions should be considered for supervisory positions.

302. If supervisors are unjust, companies will make unwise decisions.

Thoughts About Quitting

303. There are few employees who haven't thought about quitting a job. It's a tempting way to escape difficult circumstances.

304. Rarely do employees think they're going to work at a company for a brief period. They're usually looking for long tenure and growth.

305. Unforeseen developments such as supervisory injustice, nepotism, or no chance for advancement affect an employee's job satisfaction and tenure. Also, there could be personality conflicts, or too much work for too little pay. More often than not, there's a human relations difficulty an employer needs to discover and solve.

306. Whenever job problems occur, employees must decide what to do. If the company is large, departmental transfers are possible. If the company is small, is it likely the situation will change?

307. Quitting a job is a bold and permanent action. However, after looking at alternatives, it may be the best decision.

Maintaining Respect

308. Successful employers respect each employee's personality and individuality, rather than treating employees as order-taking puppets with no minds of their own.

309. If they're friendly, helpful, and don't treat employees as puppets, managers will earn the respect of employees.

310. Employees have a sense of self-worth. The more they're nurtured and their talents used, the more giving, fulfilled, and happy they'll become.

311. The more employees are allowed to grow and develop, the more loyalty they'll have to those who helped them.

312. We keep looking for buried, hidden, or deep
meanings to explain what happens to us.
We go to seminars, buy expensive books and
tapes, or put supervisors through expensive
training programs, because we're looking for some
magic management answer money can buy. All we
need to do, however, is look at how we treat our
own families. The way we treat them is the way
we'll treat co-workers. Hopefully, it's respectfully.

313. We can't buy respect; we can't demand it; we can't dictate it; we have to earn it. Then we have to maintain it, lest we lose it. Respect is hard to come by and difficult to maintain, but we can't live effectively without it; it's one of life's necessities.

 BUSINESS BRIEFS

Motivating the Stubborn Employee

314. If a task is explained in an unhurried, non-threatening, friendly way, much can be accomplished. This approach is essential for stubborn employees.

315. Giving direct, bossy, ego-shattering orders to stubborn employees won't win an employer any popularity contests. No one gets anywhere trying to break a stubborn employee.

316. The way an employer asks a question usually determines what gets done and how well.

317. If employers ask graciously, employees will respond in a happier, positive manner.

Forgetting Disagreements; Keeping Promises

318. No one's perfect.

319. Everyone has disagreements. The challenge is forgetting them and dropping any grudges.

Forgiving Bossy Behavior

320. Like employees, employers don't always have good days. They may have spouses nagging them, teenagers driving them up a wall, and pets biting them. So have a heart; lighten up!

 BUSINESS BRIEFS

321. Some bosses assert themselves by being "bossy." Arrogance, however, wears thin. Occasional memory lapses can be tolerated; failures understood; crabbiness forgiven. Our humanity bonds us.

322. Rather than get angry at the humanity of others, we should be joyful. It means they're approachable.

How to Make Volunteering Pay in the Business World

323. An opportunity volunteers overlook, is one that moves them beyond volunteering to a paying job, where they cash in on the wonderful knowledge and experience they've acquired.

324. Volunteers should add "job" after the word "volunteer," because as volunteers they held important jobs and did important work.

325. When people think of volunteering, they should keep in mind the kind of paying job they might want in the future, so they can volunteer for something related. Volunteer work builds job experience and helps develop resumes.

 BUSINESS BRIEFS

326. Opportunities for volunteers are endless. First decide the type of "for pay" career eventually wanted, then get a related volunteer job for the career experience needed.

327. Employees with volunteer experience work reliably and well, not because they're forced to, but because they've learned as volunteers to work to the best of their abilities without any monetary reward and without supervisors looking over their shoulders.

328. Volunteers make trustworthy employees, plus they're cheerful, businesslike, budget-conscious, and uncomplaining. Hire them, pay them a fair wage, and be glad they agreed to accept the job.

Staging a Burn-out

329. Burn-out affects almost everyone sometime.

330. Many employees work hard for years but never seem to have what they thought they'd have to show for it. Does it really matter?

331. If you reach job burn-out, and there's no future or fun in it anymore, start a new career. If you have a dream, pursue it.

332. Employees deserve to have "burn-out" sometime. Routines get monotonous. If change is needed, change should be made. Go for it!

Remembering Thoughtfulness

333. Courtesy and thoughtfulness are part of being nice.

334. Chances to be thoughtful at work are endless. The way one talks with co-workers, helps them, remembers special days, or simply holds the door for them, gets noticed and appreciated.

335. Thoughtfulness is good manners in action and always appropriate.

Enjoying Company Outings

336. Company outings give workers' families an opportunity to meet each other. Employers and employees interacting with families promotes mutual understanding and appreciation.

337. Life is short; too short to waste on petty bickering or hurt feelings. Whether at home or in the workplace, families need to gather and share good and bad times, because sharing is caring.

Business Policies

338. Flexibility is essential. Policies and procedures are meant to be guides. When policies don't apply anymore, it shouldn't be necessary to wait for some board of directors to meet and decide.

339. Extenuating circumstances can be good reasons for altering policies and procedures.

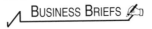

340. Company policies and procedures are meant to help employees function in an efficient manner. This doesn't mean they should never be questioned or changed.

 Business Briefs

You Know You've Worked Long Enough When . . .

341. . . . coffee breaks are coffeeless because of bladder problems.

342. . . . you and your spouse get mailings about retirement living, senior citizen insurance, and pension investing.

BUSINESS BRIEFS

343. . . . after years of paying children's college and wedding bills, the second, third and fourth mortgages on your house are finally paid off.

344. . . . you come home on time for supper one night and discover your children are grown up and gone.

345. . . . your kids leave home for good, leaving you and your spouse alone at last, but neither of you remember what you wanted to do with all your leisure time.

346. . . . your spouse finally buys you a gold chain for your neck, but huge folds of fat cover it.

347. . . . your spouse plans a retirement party for you, but you both forget to come.

348. . . . all your peers are either employed bagging groceries at the local supermarket, or working part-time at the nearby fast-food restaurant.

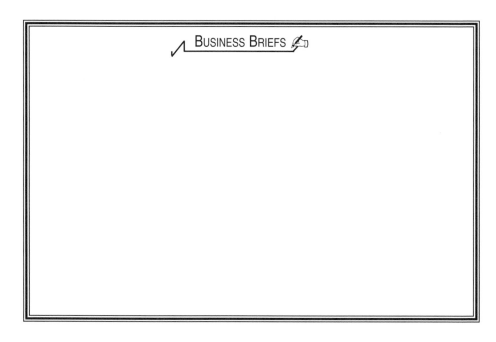

BUSINESS BRIEFS

BUSINESS BRIEFS

OTHER BOOKS AVAILABLE BY DONNA LAGORIO MONTGOMERY

Bread & Wine   ISBN 0-938577-17-4 $14.95
is a spiritual look at each person's mortality and immortality.

Tea Party   ISBN 0-938577-11-5 $14.95
shares short reflections about friendship, daily routines, and observations of life. Tuck in a purse and share with a friend at tea.

Coffee Talk   ISBN 0-938577-09-3 $14.95
includes short reflections about women, men, friendship, and families. Thoughts shared over a cup of coffee with a good friend.

Love, Life & Chocolate Chip Cookies   ISBN 0-938577-10-7 $6.95
serves up a hearty helping of wit and wisdom in short quips on children, life, and love in general.

Surviving Motherhood   ISBN 0-938577-00-X $6.95
looks at family relationships written by a mother of eight who is a survivor of motherhood herself.

Parenting a Business   ISBN 0-938577-04-2 $14.95
looks at business relationships from a parenting standpoint.

Kids + Modeling = Money   ISBN 0-13-515172-4 $9.95
is all you need to help your child begin a rewarding and prosperous modeling career. Discover the secrets of modeling success.

↗ BUSINESS BRIEFS ✍

Book Title	*Qty*	*Price*	*Total*
——————	———	———	—————
——————	———	———	—————
——————	———	———	—————
——————	———	———	—————
——————	———	———	—————
——————	———	———	—————

		Sub-total	—————
		Shipping*	—————
		Total	—————

Please make checks payable to *St. John's Publishing Inc.*

Shipping: $2.00 for first book. Add $1.00 for each additional book.

BUSINESS BRIEFS

Mail orders to:

St. John's Publishing, Inc.
6824 Oaklawn Avenue
Edina, Minnesota 55435

Please include a return address with all orders:

Name: _____

Address: _____

Phone: _____